D1126334

LUCRETIA MOTT

LUCRETIA MOTT

ABOLITIONIST & WOMEN'S RIGHTS LEADER

by Katie Marsico

Content Consultant:
Margaret H. Bacon
Author and scholar

ABDO
Publishing Company

CREDITS

Published by ABDO Publishing Company, 8000 West 78th Street, Edina, Minnesota 55439. Copyright © 2008 by Abdo Consulting Group, Inc. International copyrights reserved in all countries. No part of this book may be reproduced in any form without written permission from the publisher. The Essential Library™ is a trademark and logo of ABDO Publishing Company.

Printed in the United States.

Editor: Sara M. Hamilton
Copy Editor: Paula Lewis
Interior Design and Production: Nicole Brecke
Cover Design: Nicole Brecke

Library of Congress Cataloging-in-Publication Data
Marsico, Katie, 1980—
   Lucretia Mott / Katie Marsico.
      p. cm.
   Includes bibliographical references.
   ISBN 978-1-60453-039-1
   1. Mott, Lucretia, 1793-1880—Juvenile literature. 2. Feminists—United States—Biography—Juvenile literature. 3. Women abolitionists—United States—Biography—Juvenile literature. 4. Quakers—United States—Biography—Juvenile literature. I. Title.

   HQ1413.M68M37 2008
   305.42092—dc22
   [B]
                                        2007030759

TABLE OF CONTENTS

Chapter 1

Pennsylvania Hall burning

MAKING A STATEMENT
BY FACING THE MOB

Hundreds of angry voices rippled through what otherwise had been a quiet spring night outside Pennsylvania Hall in Philadelphia, Pennsylvania. The women attending the second Anti-Slavery Convention of American Women in

Pennsylvania Hall grew increasingly nervous as they listened to the mob outside become larger, louder, and stronger. Some of the delegates at the convention were white, and others were African American. Regardless of race, the delegates were there to support the abolitionist movement—a movement to end the institution of slavery. The delegates were aware that to accomplish such a cause, they would have to rise against fierce opposition.

On May 17, 1838, the conflict between those who opposed slavery (abolitionists) and those who supported slavery appeared to be more than a war of words. It was not unheard of for abolitionists to pay for their efforts with their lives, and the convention had sparked intense hostility in Philadelphia. Attendees of the convention had reason to fear for their safety as the mob of approximately 17,000 rioters became

Speaking to the President

Mott wanted nation-wide change, so she did not restrict her efforts to Philadelphia. In her battle to improve the rights of women and people of other races, she met with several U.S. presidents. In 1833, she spoke to President John Tyler about emancipation. In 1873, Mott visited President Ulysses S. Grant on behalf of Native Americans who were being persecuted by the government. She also dealt with former U.S. presidents, including John Quincy Adams.

increasingly violent and aggressive. Many within the mob were desperate factory workers earning a very meager wage. They feared that if the slaves were freed, their already low wage would be driven down even more through the increased competition for jobs.

Despite the hostility and danger the delegates faced, Lucretia Mott remained poised and calm. Earlier in the day, Mott reminded the other delegates to remain steadfast and strong in their fight for abolition, no matter what obstacles they would face. As one of the leaders of the convention, she was

Escorted by the Enemy

Mott not only stood her ground against people who opposed her, she also managed to get them to help her. In 1853, she headed a women's rights convention in New York City, New York. As expected, an unhappy, unsupportive crowd gathered and forced the meeting to break up early. Always calm and determined to protect others, Mott instructed her escort to help the rest of the attendees exit the building. With concern, her escort asked who would walk with her. Mott reached out and grabbed the arm of Captain Isaiah Rynders, who was the head of the mob that had disrupted the convention.

"This man will see me through," said Mott.[1] Rynders was unaware that the woman demanding his assistance was the famous and controversial Lucretia Mott. He simply saw an unimposing older woman, so he agreed to escort her. Not long after, Mott met Rynders again, and the pair had a polite conversation. After she left, someone informed the gang leader that he had just spoken to Mott. Despite this revelation, Rynders conceded that she "seemed like a good, sensible woman."[2] Like so many of her opponents, he could not help but acknowledge Mott's admirable character.

not about to give up the struggle for social reform simply because others disagreed with her or called for her to be silent.

The United States was not quite 62 years old, and its citizens were still shaping its identity. Would the country allow one human being to own another? Would leaders make freedom the law of the land? Should only men receive a complete education and aspire to professional careers? Should women also have the same opportunities and rights? Mott was convinced that equality would never win out if people abandoned the argument for it every time they were scared or threatened.

Mott felt responsible for the brave women who had come forth to attend the convention. They could not stay inside Pennsylvania Hall forever, and there was just as good a chance the mob would make its way into the building even if they did.

Equality at All Times

Mott did not expect special treatment from anyone because she was a female abolitionist. When she visited Delaware in 1840, a pro-slavery mob attacked her friend Daniel Neall. As he was taken from the home where Mott was staying, she argued with the men to take her instead, insisting, "I ask no courtesy at your hands on account of my sex."[3] The men did not agree to her request. Ultimately, they tarred and feathered Neall, but they did not harm him as badly as they might have if she had not intervened.

Pennsylvania Hall

The burning of Pennsyl-
vania Hall was disap-
pointing to many local
abolitionists, but the struc-
ture had special meaning
for Mott and her husband,
James. They had raised a
large amount of money
for construction of the
building, which was cre-
ated as a place for people
to discuss issues such
as the social injustice of
slavery. Pennsylvania Hall
featured meeting rooms,
galleries, and a book-
store that offered reading
materials related to abolition. It had been formally
open only three days be-
fore it was set on fire.

Adding more tension to the situation was the fact that females were speaking out on such a sensitive issue. In the early 1800s, many people in the United States still believed that women had no place outside of kitchens or parlors. To many, women were expected to remain quiet and to not speak publicly on such controversial issues as slavery.

Those who held such beliefs were angered that the delegates at the convention challenged their views. These were the kind of people Mott faced as she prepared members of the convention to exit the hall. She calmly instructed the ladies to walk out in pairs—each white woman would leave arm-in-arm with an African-American attendee.

After members of the convention exited, Philadelphia's mayor made a brief appearance and pleaded with the crowd to keep the peace, but he

Pennsylvania Hall in ruins

left shortly thereafter. Like many public officials, he was hesitant to become involved in the heated debate surrounding abolition. Once the mayor left, the mob broke into Pennsylvania Hall and proceeded to burn it to the ground. Soon after, the hall was in ruins.

After the burning of Pennsylvania Hall, the mob threatened to burn down Mott's home before going on to terrorize the African-American community. Thanks to some quick thinking by a family friend, the mob did not end up burning Mott's house. But even if they had, Mott undoubtedly would have continued her many social crusades. As she once stated,

> *I have no idea of submitting tamely to injustice. … I will oppose it with all the moral powers with which I am endowed. I am no advocate of passivity.*[4]

"On to the Motts'!"

Mott's home barely escaped being vandalized during the second Anti-Slavery Convention of American Women. As the mob tore across Philadelphia the night of May 17, 1838, they burned buildings and terrorized the African-American community. Luckily for Lucretia, the Mott family had many good friends who respected her outspoken nature and bold beliefs. One such acquaintance went unnoticed as he blended in with the hostile crowd. By the time Mott's enemies reached her front porch, he shouted out "On to the Motts'!"[5] and managed to confuse the mob into thinking they were at the wrong house and to move on.

Lucretia Coffin Mott

The Coffins' home on Nantucket Island

A Taste of Equality on Nantucket Island

Though she would one day travel to bustling, crowded cities to preach her message of peace and equality, Lucretia never lost her fondness for Nantucket Island—where she was born on January 3, 1793. Approximately 30 miles (48 km) south of

Cape Cod, Massachusetts, the town of Nantucket was home to boat builders, fishermen, and traders. Many of its residents belonged to the Religious Society of Friends—also known as Quakers. Most people on the island knew each other and several were related.

The Quakers, who had first arrived on Nantucket in 1659, believed that obedience and simplicity were the best ways to invite positive change. Lucretia's parents, Thomas Coffin Jr. and Anna Folger Coffin, shared these beliefs. Lucretia was taught from an early age that God shared His wisdom with people through "an Inward Light that illuminated their consciences."[1] In the Quaker faith, everyone was born with the Inward Light. Therefore, everyone was equal.

Most Quakers avoided outward decoration of any kind, including on clothing, because they feared it might affect their ability to reflect spiritually and focus on God. When

The History of Nantucket

Nantucket is approximately 15 miles (24 km) long and between three and six miles (5 and 10 km) wide. Initially, the island belonged to Wampanoag Native Americans but it was ultimately claimed by English colonists. Beginning in about 1641, Nantucket was governed by the New York Colony. Quakers began settling there in the 1690s, and in 1692, the island became a part of the Massachusetts Colony. Nantucket was famous for the whalers, fishermen, boat builders, and traders who used its port. Today, the island's economy is based mostly on tourism.

Lucretia attended religious meetings on Sundays and Thursdays, she saw a gathering of men and women who dressed simply in black, gray, and white. No one sang, and sometimes there was little talking. As a rule, Quakers only spoke during meetings when they were inspired to do so.

Spiritual leaders, known as elders, were responsible for ensuring that other Quakers remained centered on their commitment to God and led moral lives. Because Quakers believed that God spoke to people regardless of their gender, both men and women served as elders. This type of equality was not common or well accepted outside the Quaker communities in the late 1700s, when women had few roles in society besides as wives and mothers. For Nantucket Islanders, however, life did not allow homemakers such as Anna Coffin to sit back and wait for men to tell them what to do. Her

The Origin of the Name *Quaker*

In 1647, George Fox, an English preacher, founded the Religious Society of Friends, whose members later became known as Quakers. Fox claimed the name *Quaker* came about because he had once told a judge that he "should tremble at the word of the Lord."[2] Another possible origin of the name was that people who belonged to the religion were known to quake, or quiver and shake, due to the strong emotions they experienced during religious meetings.

George Fox, Quaker founder, preaching to a woman

husband, Thomas, was a sea captain and was often
away on voyages for several months at a time. This
left Anna—and Lucretia—with many important
responsibilities and decisions to make.

HELPING RUN THE HOUSEHOLD

While Thomas was at sea, it was up to Anna to look after their children. Like other women on the island, she was left to make weighty decisions about everything from parenting to finances. Anna also ran a shop out of the Coffins' parlor, where she sold food and household items. This helped bring in money while Thomas was away.

Lucretia had an older sister named Sarah and four younger siblings—Elizabeth ("Eliza"), Thomas, Mary, and Martha. The Coffins

Enacting the Part of Men

Later in life, Lucretia remembered Nantucket as more than a scenic seaside community. Because so many of the island's male residents were often away on ocean voyages, she grew up in a society where it was natural for women to work, manage a home, and share the same day-to-day activities as men. In a letter written to women's rights leader Elizabeth Cady Stanton in March 1855, Lucretia wrote:

During the absence of their husbands, Nantucket women have been compelled to transact business. … This has made them adept in trade. They have kept their own accounts, and indeed enacted the part of men.[3]

After life on Nantucket, Lucretia was shocked to discover that the rest of the United States was not as broad-minded and encouraging when it came to notions of equality. While many of her mid-nineteenth-century counterparts might have considered it improper for women to display such independence and spirit, she viewed the attitude on Nantucket as practical and healthy. During a speech, she noted, "The exercise of women's talents … tended to develop their intellectual powers and strengthen them mentally and physically."[4]

had another child, Lydia, who died at an early age. Lucretia was expected to do her share of the household chores. Sarah, who was more than two years older than Lucretia, was disabled, so extra duties fell on Lucretia as the second-oldest child. At the age of four, Lucretia began attending a local Quaker school. When she was not in class, she assisted her mother by running errands, sewing, cooking, and cleaning.

Mother and daughter shared a close and loving relationship that endured throughout their lives. Years later, in a letter to a friend, Lucretia described her mother fondly, writing,"She was companionable in every way ... her children delighted in her society."[5]

Though Lucretia was a spirited child, her mother taught her the importance of patience, organization, and self-discipline. Lucretia's mother demonstrated confidence and independence—two traits that Lucretia ultimately became famous for and encouraged other women to develop.

Like her mother, Lucretia was intelligent. Though Nantucket and the Quaker philosophy offered more social equality than was typical for the late eighteenth century, the young girl was aware of the injustices and the inequalities of the outside world, including slavery.

VALUES FORMED AND A FAMILY REUNITED

Although Quakers did not allow slave ships to dock in Nantucket Harbor, Lucretia was still able to witness how the slave trade was a profitable business for nearby seaports. Lucretia learned in school about the horrors that African men, women, and children were regularly exposed to on their journeys from their homelands to the Americas. She was sickened by the accounts of people who were separated from their families and sometimes viciously killed.

But it seemed there was little she could do with her anger. Students read, recited, and practiced simple mathematics. They did not talk about important or controversial issues of the day. Nonetheless, Lucretia decided early on that the cruelty of slavery had no place in the United States or any other part of the world.

First Lessons on Slavery

In school, Lucretia read about the slave trade in *Mental Improvement*, by British Quaker Priscilla Wakefield. Lucretia and her classmates learned how Africans on slave ships had little space and fresh air and often died early deaths. One line stayed with her for many years: "Humanity shudders at your account."[6] Lucretia would never understand or accept that one human being could treat another with such cruelty.

Such injustice as slavery may have sparked the young girl's fierce desire to speak out and improve society. But before she tackled other people's problems, she had to cope with the pain and worry that had settled on her own home by 1802. Only nine years old at the time, Lucretia eagerly awaited the return of her father, who was due back from a whaling expedition. The Coffins were relieved every time Thomas returned from a voyage at sea. Whaling was not easy work and, occasionally, it cost men their lives. Lucretia's father could only guess at when he would make his way back to Nantucket. The family frequently rushed to the harbor whenever a whaling ship docked. As 1802 progressed, however, they were repeatedly disappointed. Though cheerful, hardworking, and faith-filled, Lucretia's mother, Anna, was understandably distressed. January of 1803 marked nearly three years of her husband's continued absence. Anna, though, never neglected her duties at home or in the shop, and Lucretia did her best to lighten her mother's spirits and help her with the heavy load of chores they shared.

Finally, on a winter morning in 1803, Thomas unexpectedly appeared at their home on Fair Street. Amid the excitement and emotions that followed his arrival, he explained the reason for his extended trip. His ship had sailed along the coast of South America and was captured by the Spanish, who forced him to dock the ship in Chile. His vessel was confiscated, so he traveled by foot over the Andes Mountains and eventually boarded a boat in Brazil that was bound for the United States.

As Lucretia listened to her father's adventures and saw her mother's tremendous relief, the ten-year-old witnessed two people who had remained courageous and determined in the face of both physical and spiritual challenges. Their reunion was evidence that one should never give up hope, even when confronted with sadness and almost certain defeat. Though life would soon lead her off the island, memories such as this one helped Lucretia recognize her own inner strength, as well as the incredible changes that strength might help her accomplish. ⌐

"Spitfire"

It was not always easy for young Lucretia to live up to her religion's demands for patience, silence, and obedience. With a quick mind and just as quick of a temper, she earned the nickname "Spitfire" from her classmates. She always seemed to have a sharp answer waiting for those people who could not match her intelligence or expectations. Her own mother remarked that she liked "to give as good as she got."[7]

A nineteenth-century whaling ship

*Elias Hicks, Quaker minister and cofounder
of Nine Partners boarding school*

A Life-altering
Education

eeking a somewhat safer career than
whaling, Thomas Coffin became
a merchant and moved his family to Boston,
Massachusetts in 1804. As was the case in so many
other major American cities, Boston public schools

placed an emphasis on educating boys. Classes for girls were held only half of the year and usually did not continue past grammar school. Boys had the opportunity to attend classes more frequently and often pursued an education past the eighth grade.

Many people thought this system made sense. After all, girls would eventually marry, have children, and be responsible for cooking, cleaning, and other household duties. At that time, it was the men who became doctors, lawyers, and political leaders. Thomas and Anna did not support this philosophy. As Lucretia later recalled, "My father had a desire to make his daughters useful."[1] In July 1806, the Coffins sent Lucretia and Eliza to Nine Partners, a Quaker boarding school in Dutchess County, New York. Though girls and boys lived in separate areas and attended separate classes, they learned the same lessons and spent the same amount of time in school.

OLD FEELINGS, NEW INSPIRATIONS

Although rules were strict at Nine Partners, Lucretia enjoyed her time there. She immediately proved to her teachers and classmates that she had a powerful memory and a quick mind. Lucretia also enjoyed the occasional visitors and guest speakers who gave presentations. She was particularly moved by the sermons of Elias Hicks. Hicks had helped found the school and had passionate opinions on a subject already dear to Lucretia's heart—slavery.

Quakers were a peaceful people famous for their opposition to slavery. After the Revolutionary War (1775-1783), the United States was a new nation determining its position on a variety of issues. The topic of abolition divided both citizens and politicians. As the debate grew more heated, many Quakers became less outspoken and more hesitant to even discuss slavery. Hicks was convinced this reaction was a mistake. Though several members of his religion considered his views extreme, Lucretia wholeheartedly agreed with him. She found that his sermons only further inspired her compassion, pity, and anger on behalf of slaves.

"… it is a most necessary and important Christian duty, for all those who are either directly or indirectly concerned in the slavery of their fellow creatures … to consider the manner and way in which the slavery of the Africans was first introduced; and by what means it has been so long continued; not doubting … that it was first introduced by fraud and force, and continued by an unjust and tyrannical power; and will, therefore, be induced to restore to them their just and native rights, as free men, which no law nor power of men or nations ought to deprive them of without their consent."[2]

—Elias Hicks

Another inspiring figure at Nine Partners was James Mott Sr., who managed the school and also held strong anti-slavery views. Lucretia became close friends with his granddaughter Sarah and eagerly accepted an invitation to the Motts' home in Mamaroneck, New York, in 1806.

Sarah had four brothers and sisters. One of her brothers, James, was a "tall, blond, serious young man, who rarely said much."[3] Five years older than Lucretia, he taught boys at Nine Partners. Initially, the two had little reason to speak to one another or spend any time together. Yet their relationship— among several

Obedience at Any Cost?

"I ... always loved the good [and] in childhood desired to do the right,"[4] Lucretia proclaimed as an adult. However, sometimes "doing the right" meant going against the strict orders of her Quaker teachers. A few rules were challenging for Lucretia, yet she tried her best to respect authority at Nine Partners.

Some rules, however, went too far in Lucretia's opinion. She found it difficult to blindly obey her teachers in every instance. The boarding school took special efforts to keep girls and boys apart. The two groups were instructed and housed in separate areas. They were rarely allowed to intermingle. Yet when Lucretia heard that the staff was scolding a boy by locking him in a closet and depriving him of his dinner, she had to take action. Lucretia and her sister Eliza decided to sneak to the part of the school used by male students and pass food underneath the closet door to the boy. Although they escaped without being caught and punished, Lucretia set a pattern that would continue for the rest of her life. In the future, she would risk her own safety to help others who were treated unfairly.

other things in Lucretia's life—would soon change as she grew from an impatient, sharp-tongued girl into a determined and dedicated woman.

An Attachment Formed at Boarding School

By 1808, 15-year-old Lucretia had completed all of her classes and had earned the admiration of much of the staff at Nine Partners. The school realized how talented and intelligent the young woman was and asked her to stay on as an assistant teacher. Lucretia agreed but soon found herself irritated by a situation involving none other than the serious and handsome James Mott.

Much to her dissatisfaction, Lucretia discovered that the young man was being paid more than twice as much as Deborah Rodgers, the older and more qualified teacher who she assisted.

Lit by an Inner Fire

Though there are no formal portraits of Lucretia as a young woman, historians suspect that she was attractive and that her appearance revealed some of her inner spirit. In the words of biographer Margaret Hope Bacon: "Her eyes were hazel and deeply set under finely arched brows. Her skin was white, her cheeks pink, her mouth rosy. Though small and slender, she had a rounded figure and a narrow waist. ... She was often laughing and chattering, lit by an inner fire. Even when she was quiet, an amused smile lurked at the corners of her mouth."[5]

There was not much she could do
to correct the situation. Nevertheless,
Lucretia considered it completely
unacceptable that equally experienced
men and women should earn
different wages—especially if they had
the same position and did the same
amount of work. She realized that,
just as Rodgers, she could be denied
fair treatment merely on account of
her gender.

Despite her anger, Lucretia
understood the incident had very
little to do with James and much
more to do with society in general. By
1809, the pair had grown closer. Her
fiery spirit and his solemn stillness
seemed to balance each other for
the better. That same year, however,
Lucretia's father bought a nail factory
in Philadelphia and moved his family
there. Lucretia left Nine Partners
when her father requested that she
join the family at their new house.

Training to Usefulness

Although Lucretia worked
as an assistant teacher at
Nine Partners, she was
not offered a salary. Her
compensation for work-
ing was the experience
she would gain. Both Lu-
cretia and her parents saw
it as important for her to
remain at Nine Partners.
As she later recalled: "My
father was … in success-
ful business in Boston;
but with his views of the
importance of training
a woman to usefulness,
he and my mother gave
their consent to another
year being devoted to that
institution."[6]

"Is This Really a Wedding?"

As was the custom of Quakers in the nineteenth century, James and Lucretia did not have an elaborate marriage ceremony. They exchanged vows during the standard weekly worship. People dressed plainly. Even the bride wore gray. Bright colors and festive songs went against Quakers' beliefs, as they feared worldly distractions might take attention away from God and the Inward Light. Vows were brief and to the point—with God's help, Lucretia and James promised to be loving and faithful to each other. The adults present understood the reason for this simple, straightforward approach. Yet Lucretia's five-year-old sister, Martha, could not help but watch the proceedings and innocently ask, "Is this really a wedding?"[8]

Though Philadelphia was home to more Quakers than Boston, it still did not provide the close-knit atmosphere of Nantucket. It was also missing what Lucretia had sadly left behind in New York—James, whom she later affectionately referred to as "an attachment formed while at boarding school."[7] To her great joy, however, her father offered to make the young man a business partner if he came to Philadelphia. James accepted the offer and both sets of parents gladly granted Lucretia and James permission to marry. After a formal approval by local Quaker authorities, the couple wed on April 10, 1811. The simple ceremony marked the beginning of a 56-year union that provided Lucretia with infinite support and encouragement during her famous career as a social reformer.

James and Lucretia Mott

A Quaker meeting in nineteenth-century Philadelphia

WIFE, MOTHER,
QUAKER MINISTER

No matter how much she and James loved each other, 18-year-old Lucretia had a new life in Philadelphia that was filled with its share of hardships. As was customary of the time, the newlyweds moved in with her parents, the Coffins.

By August 1811, James and Lucretia were able to purchase their own home on Union Street and began attending the Twelfth Street Meeting.

While Lucretia enjoyed married life, she worried about her parents. Her father's factory was not doing well. Money was so tight that the Coffins finally realized they could no longer afford to keep their house on Second Street. That autumn, they moved in with James and Lucretia. They were present the following August when the young couple welcomed their first baby, Anna.

Since James worked for Lucretia's father, their careers and finances were unavoidably intertwined. Business continued to suffer and was further impacted by the War of 1812 (1812-1814), which was being fought between Great Britain and the United States. In late 1813, Lucretia discovered she was pregnant again. The young couple briefly moved to

Out and About

In the early 1800s, it was customary for new mothers to stay inside and rest for four to six weeks after the birth of a baby. Lucretia, however, was an active, energetic woman who had many responsibilities and little patience to remain in bed while there was work to be done. Much to the shock and surprise of Philadelphia society, she was active just days after Anna's birth. As Lucretia later joked, "[I was] classified among the Indians for so rash an act."[1]

Mamaroneck, New York, where James hoped to earn more money at his uncle's cotton mill.

Despite their economic troubles, Lucretia and James rejoiced in the birth of their first son, Thomas ("Tommy"), who was born in July of 1814. By October, Lucretia and James were back in Philadelphia after James accepted a job in a plow store. Their constant moving and seemingly endless financial worries concerned Lucretia. But she tried to see some benefit to their difficult beginnings. As she remarked years later,

A Mother's Gentle Touch and a Teacher's Wise Approach

Lucretia was an avid reader and especially enjoyed books that furthered her knowledge or caused her to reflect on her own life, attitudes, and opinions. Lucretia particularly enjoyed a book written by her husband's grandfather, James Mott Sr., titled, *Observations on Education*. The book encouraged adults to teach children in a gentle, loving manner, as opposed to using harsh punishment and discipline.

Lucretia agreed with the ideas expressed in the book. Like many other members of her religion, she supported the belief that children were born with a pure heart and shared a direct communication with God, as did adults. Lucretia believed knowledge and compassion were better teaching tools than scolding or condemning. As she later preached,

We should never teach children that they have wicked hearts ... or that it is easier to do wrong than right, they will soon learn that it is easier to do right than wrong. Children love peace. The little child knows when it says, mother, I love everybody. There is a Divine instinct in them which prompts to this feeling.[2]

These trials ... were not without their good effect in disciplining the mind, and leading it to set a just estimate on worldly pleasures."³

Overcoming Challenges, Crippled by Tragedy

Lucretia was glad to be reunited with her family in late 1814, but she could not help feeling frustrated with her father for not having paid more attention to her mother's wisdom. Anna had voiced her misgivings when Thomas decided to lend money to a friend. Now the man could not pay Thomas back, and the Coffins were $9,000 in debt. Lucretia's disappointment in her father quickly turned to grief. In 1815, Thomas died from typhus.

Though stinging from the tragedy of her loss, Lucretia's mother forged ahead and successfully started her own shop in Philadelphia. Within a few years, both Lucretia's mother

Money Matters

After her father's death, Lucretia's mother took full responsibility for the sum total of her husband's debt. As Lucretia recalled in an 1871 letter to her sister Martha, "... one of our noble Mother's first acts, as a widow, was to destroy that note."⁴ Following her father's passing, Lucretia was upset by the fact that wives so often suffered on account of their husbands' financial mistakes. However, she admired her mother's display of independence and use of common sense when it came to money matters.

and the Motts seemed to be getting back on their feet. By March 1817, Lucretia had begun teaching at a school for girls, which was run by a relative. James was employed with a local merchant.

Their prosperity was, once again, to be brutally interrupted. In April, Lucretia and Tommy became sick with a fever. Older and stronger, Lucretia recovered in a few days, but her son never did. His death left the normally passionate and opinionated 24-year-old Lucretia facing the greatest and most painful challenge of her life.

EARNING RESPECT AND GROWING MORE OUTSPOKEN

After Tommy's death, Lucretia looked to her faith for comfort. Over time, she recaptured some of her spirit and enthusiasm but had a difficult time grasping the purpose behind the loss. Why had God taken

Equality Even in Words

Though not as common today, "plain speech" was used among nineteenth-century Quakers and included words such as thee and thou ("you") and thy and thine ("your" or "yours"). Since Quakers advocated the idea of equality, plain speech made more sense than Mr., Mrs., or any other title that created a distinction of class or gender. "Plain speech" ensured that everyone—whether they were male or female, rich or poor—was addressed in the same manner.

Quakers on their way to a Monthly Meeting

her child's life? Lucretia intently read the Bible.
She hoped to find answers within the scriptures.
Even with the birth of her daughter Maria in 1818,
the joy she experienced did not end her struggle to
find acceptance and inner peace after such a loss. As
time passed, her deep contemplation about personal

struggles led her to break the silence one Sunday in 1818 at the Twelfth Street Meeting. She voiced her realization that people could survive the difficult times in life if they put their entire trust in God's limitless power,

> As all our efforts to resist temptation and overcome the world prove fruitless, unless aided by Thy Holy Spirit, enable us to approach Thy Throne, and ask of Thee the blessing of Thy preservation from all evil, that we may be wholly devoted to Thee and Thy glorious cause.[5]

The gathering was impressed and invited her to speak during meetings more often if she was moved to do so. Lucretia accepted this encouragement and continued to impress her fellow Quakers with her sensible and inspiring revelations. By January 1821, she gained formal recognition as a Quaker minister. While some may have considered her young for such a title, 28-year-old Lucretia's common sense and obvious devotion proved that the honor was deserved.

This new role did not mean that she stopped voicing her opinions or unquestioningly agreed with the actions of Quaker elders. Lucretia especially disapproved of the increasing number of Quakers who were being disowned by the Religious Society of Friends. The disownment process involved denying a disobedient member any connection with the group. Elders sometimes inflicted punishment by cutting connections with offenders and informing them that they were no longer welcome or accepted at the Monthly Meeting. From Lucretia's perspective, their reaction was often unfair.

She passionately defended members whom she felt had been disowned unjustly. Often their "crimes" ranged from attending the wedding of a relative who married outside of the faith to attending lectures on educational reform that elders considered radical. In defending such members, Lucretia put both herself and James at risk for disownment as well. Many elders were unhappy that Lucretia spoke out against their actions. As she

The Responsibilities of a Quaker Minister

As a Quaker minister, Lucretia served as an example to members of the Twelfth Street Meeting. Even with the solemn silence that characterized Quaker services, it was accepted that ministers spoke more frequently and exercised authority. Ministers were responsible for gathering with elders to discuss issues related to their Monthly Meeting. Some members became Public Friends who traveled to spread their religious message and visited Quaker communities. Lucretia eventually took up active ministry as a Public Friend during the early 1830s.

eventually recounted, "My husband [and I] came close to 'losing our place' by uttering our indignant protest against their intolerance."[6] Though she realized what was at stake, Lucretia worried about how the Religious Society of Friends would maintain its membership if it continued turning out people whom she described as some of its most "active, benevolent citizens."[7]

By the mid—1820s, it was becoming clear that the young minister's opinions on disownment were merely one source of internal conflict within the Quaker community. The horrors of slavery and the prospect of abolition were both intense and sensitive topics that called into question people's political ideas, religious beliefs, and views on humanity. For some, it was easier and more comfortable to simply avoid these issues. Lucretia, however, knew where she stood and was unafraid to speak her mind. ⁓

Quakers at worship services

Slaves picking cotton in the fields

COURAGE AMID
CONTROVERSY

The 1820s were a time of change and
progress for the Coffins and the Motts.
Lucretia gave birth to three more children—another
son named Thomas in 1823, Elizabeth in 1825,
and Martha ("Pattie") in 1828. Lucretia's mother

had boldly moved from keeping a shop to running a boardinghouse to eventually helping manage a Quaker school in New York. James enjoyed financial success after breaking into the wholesale business. His profits and Lucretia's careful saving allowed them to purchase a new house in Philadelphia on Sansom Street in 1824.

While Lucretia might have experienced great happiness at home, she remained shaken by the cruelty and conflict that characterized the outside world. Pennsylvania was a free state, meaning it did not allow residents to own slaves. Nevertheless, Philadelphia was affected by the growing controversy surrounding the abolition of slavery. At the most basic level, everyday life for many African-American residents was far from easy. Free blacks often struggled with discrimination and poverty. Such men and women had little hope of a promising future while slavery and inequality existed.

A Sense of Resourcefulness

By 1825, six children and two adults lived in the Motts' home on Sansom Street. This included Lucretia's orphaned niece, Anna. To run such a large, busy household, Lucretia used excellent organizational skills and resourcefulness. She was an excellent cook, frequently serving Nantucket delicacies such as pickled herring and blackberry pudding. She also proved that she had her mother's quick mind when it came to money matters. By mending linens and flipping carpets to use them longer, Lucretia made sure that every item in the house was put to its greatest possible use.

FIFTY DOLLARS
REWARD.

Ran away from Mount Welby, Prince George's County, Maryland, on Monday, the 2d inst., a negro man calling himself Joe Bond, about 25 years of age, about 5 feet 6 inches in height, stout built, copper complexion; the only mark recollected is a peculiar speck in one of his eyes. Had on when he went away a frock tweed coat, dark brown, and cap near the same color. I will give twenty-five dollars if taken in Prince George's County, Md., or in Alexandria County, Virginia; and fifty dollars if taken elsewhere and returned to me, or secured so that I get him again.

T. R. EDELAN

Piscataway, Prince George's, December 5, 1850.

Throughout the 1800s, many slaves would attempt to escape to the free states in the North.

Philadelphia was also the destination for many slaves who tried to escape from their Southern masters. Escaped slaves traveled to the Northern city in search of freedom. Free African Americans were also at risk. Kidnappers, eager to make a profit, pulled free African Americans off the streets and forced them onto Southern auction blocks to be sold into bondage.

The issue of abolition created mixed feelings within Philadelphia's Quaker community as well. The ideas of liberty and racial equality were good in theory, but many Northern states still had business dealings connected to Southern plantations and slave labor. Much to her dismay, Lucretia realized that she and her husband were not guiltless in this regard.

FAMILY EFFORTS TO END SLAVERY

As James was a Philadelphia merchant, both he and Lucretia were disturbed to know that a great deal of his profits came from cotton products, such as clothing and writing paper. Lucretia had visited Virginia in 1818 and witnessed the inhumane conditions that slaves endured. The fact that her family was making money off items linked to slavery was a brutal awakening for her.

She pleaded with James to sell wool products instead, but he was concerned. James hesitated at the idea of cutting off a major source of his success and financial security, even if the thought of slavery morally repulsed him. In the mid—1820s, James was not ready to take the risk, but the couple found other ways to fight slavery.

James and Lucretia decided that they could at least boycott certain products connected to slavery, even if it was only within the walls of their own home. Within their home on Sansom Street, items such as molasses, sugar, cotton clothes, cotton linens, and paper with cotton content were not allowed.

Their sacrifice was neither simple nor easy. The family, however, believed in the reason behind the boycott and was willing to abandon small pleasures for a much greater cause. James even played an influential role in creating the Philadelphia Free Produce Society in 1826. This group educated consumers about the benefits of buying from stores whose products were not connected to slave labor.

The Profit of a Wife's Advice

"I confess I should be much better satisfied, if they could do business that was in no wise dependent on slavery, and perhaps some will appear after a while."[1] Lucretia repeatedly told others how she often begged James to stop selling cotton products. Though initially reluctant, in 1830, he ultimately fulfilled his wife's wish. James quickly discovered how wise the decision had been—both as a businessman and a social reformer—when he found that wool brought in just as substantial of a profit.

Lucretia used her influence as a Quaker minister to speak in favor of the boycott of slave products at the Twelfth Street Meeting. Several Quaker members agreed with her antislavery sentiments. Many participated in the boycott as well. Yet elders wondered if her approach was appropriate. Meetings were to be devoted to religious matters. They did not approve of her using sermons to gain support for her increasing activities as an abolitionist. Soon, however, Quaker leaders would find themselves locking horns with Lucretia over issues unrelated to slavery and directly linked to a developing conflict within the Religious Society of Friends.

DIFFICULT DECISIONS AND A PAINFUL PARTING

Elias Hicks, the man who had inspired Lucretia when she was a student, was now threatening to

A Sweet Rhyme for a Not-So-Sweet Candy

Every time consumers purchased candy from free-produce stores, they were reminded of the difference they made by supporting the boycott. Upon unwrapping each treat, a person was greeted with the following rhyme: "Take this, my friend, you must not fear to eat. No slave hath toiled to cultivate this sweet."[2] The clever poem was one way of compensating for the way the candies—which were made without sugar—tasted.

create a crack within the Quaker community. Hicks spoke passionately about how Quakers were moving away from a personal relationship with God and relying too heavily on restrictive rules and overly powerful elders. He encouraged people to be open to new ideas and not become trapped in outdated traditions. Orthodox Quakers rejected Hicks's philosophy. They worried that he was undervaluing the importance of Holy Scripture and labeled him as a radical.

Before long, the Religious Society of Friends was divided between

Determined to Act, Despite Disapproval

Lucretia was fully aware that not everyone—especially certain elders at the Twelfth Street Meeting—agreed with her outspoken methods of promoting abolition. The personal criticism and controversy were difficult, but she recognized that there were greater issues at stake than the elders' approval of her. As she noted,

> I am aware of the place I stand; I know there are many who will not allow anything to be said in behalf of the slave. But I believe it to be my duty to plead the cause of the poor and of the oppressed whether they will hear or whether they will forbear.[3]

It would have been easy enough for a nineteenth-century homemaker to feel satisfied about her personal boycott of cotton and sugar and to merely express her opinions over the family dinner table. But to Lucretia, every U.S. citizen had a responsibility to take a stand against slavery. Otherwise, they were no better than the plantation owners and slave traders. "The crime is national," she emphasized. "We are all involved in it. ... We are called to bear our testimony against sin, of whatever form, in whatever way presented."[4]

Orthodox members and more liberal Quakers, known as "Hicksites." Both groups valued Lucretia for her spirit, speaking abilities, and intelligence. She was an important and respected figure within the Quaker community. Inevitably, whatever side she chose would have an impact on what other people thought.

For Lucretia, it seemed impossible to make a decision. James favored Hicksites, while relatives from both their families and most members of the Twelfth Street Meeting supported Orthodox Quakers. By late 1827, she made her decision and joined the Hicksites at the Cherry Street Meeting (which later became the Race Street Meeting).

Lucretia regretted the painful split that separated her from people who had carried her through several crises and encouraged her in her ministry. But Lucretia believed in the need for a more open-minded view toward

Changing Opinions, Changing Schools

Lucretia's support of the Hicksites did more than affect her personal standing at the Twelfth Street Meeting—it also impacted her children's education. In 1826, her daughter Anna had been sent to a school run by Orthodox Quakers. After Lucretia's break from that group in 1827, it was obvious that other plans would have to be made. Lucretia sent Anna and Maria to the boarding school where her mother was working in Aurora, New York.

change. She had long opposed some of the ways in which elders clung to rigid traditions and handed down discipline. As she noted many years later,

> *True religion and freedom of thought seem to be so inseparable that I cannot make the comparison that it is better to be free than to be religious. Religion and freedom must go together.*[5]

CAUTION!!

COLORED PEOPLE

OF BOSTON, ONE & ALL,

You are hereby respectfully **CAUTIONED** and advised, to avoid conversing with the

Watchmen and Police Officers of Boston,

For since the recent **ORDER OF THE MAYOR & ALDERMEN**, they are empowered to act as

KIDNAPPERS

AND

Slave Catchers,

And they have already been actually employed in **KIDNAPPING, CATCHING, AND KEEPING SLAVES.** Therefore, if you value your **LIBERTY**, and the *Welfare of the Fugitives* among you, *Shun* them in every possible manner, as so many *HOUNDS* on the track of the most unfortunate of your race.

Keep a Sharp Look Out for KIDNAPPERS, and have TOP EYE open.

Throughout the 1800s, posters warned free African Americans of kidnappers.

Antislavery emblem that Lucretia Mott often used as her own seal

THE VOICE OF WOMEN IN THE WAR FOR FREEDOM

The Motts quickly gained a reputation for hospitality at their large home on Sansom Street. Abolitionists and other social reformers frequently visited. One such visitor was young William Lloyd Garrison, an antislavery journalist who first spent time with the Motts in 1830. With the Motts' encouragement, Garrison founded the New England Anti-Slavery Society in 1832. He again called upon the Motts in December 1833 when he arranged a convention in Philadelphia to create a national group that would become the American Anti-Slavery Society.

During the early stages of the American Anti-Slavery Society, Lucretia often hosted delegates in her home on Sansom Street. At one point, she served high tea to 50 delegates. Her organizational abilities and superb cooking skills were an asset, but she wanted to contribute more. Women's opinions were rarely sought at important political gatherings. Yet, on this occasion, Lucretia was pleasantly surprised. On December 5, she and a few female relatives were invited to the society's meeting in Philadelphia.

Friendly Advice

Lucretia and Garrison quickly became friends after their first meeting. She admired his spirit and drive. He respected her quick mind and sense of compassion. The Quaker minister often gave the young journalist advice about delivering speeches, as well as constructive criticism regarding the tone of his articles in the *Liberator*—an antislavery newspaper Garrison first published in 1831.

Lucretia, her mother, and her daughter Anna eagerly attended the remainder of the convention. There they learned how the society planned to educate the public about the need to end slavery. One of the group's suggestions was that women create their own antislavery societies—an idea that Lucretia wasted no time putting into action.

On December 9, 1833, she and approximately 30 other women met at a schoolhouse to form the Philadelphia Female Anti-Slavery Society.

From Simple Grammar to Serious Sentiments

When Lucretia was asked to attend the American Anti-Slavery Society convention in December 1833, she had no intention of doing anything other than listening to the proceedings. As time progressed, she began to speak her mind on a few minor points. At first, her polite suggestions focused on basic grammatical corrections to a document called the Declaration of Sentiments, which summed up the goals and agenda of the society.

By the end of the convention, though, she had begun to express herself on much larger issues than the way something was phrased. To Lucretia's great shock and dismay, several abolitionists hesitated to sign the Declaration of Sentiments. The society planned to take steps in educating the public about the need to immediately end slavery, as well as racism in general. Some delegates considered the plans too controversial and worried how their signatures would affect their reputations.

Not only did Lucretia ask James to sign his name—she also addressed all those gathered, "If our principles are right, why should we be cowards? Why should we wait for those who never had the courage to maintain the inalienable rights of the slave?"[1] Her words gave many delegates the confidence they needed to step forward and formally attach their names to the newly founded organization.

This society included white and African-American members. The group's constitution, which Lucretia helped write, clearly stated its purpose: "We deem it our duty ... to manifest our abhorrence of the ... injustice and deep sin of slavery by united and vigorous exertions."[2] It did not take long for Lucretia to recognize how much hostility these exertions would spark.

SPREADING THE WORD IN AN UNFRIENDLY WORLD

Lucretia's work with the Philadelphia Female Anti-Slavery Society kept her busy. Members participated in committees that helped escaped slaves and protected free African Americans from kidnappers hoping to smuggle them back to slave states. The society also sponsored local efforts to benefit Philadelphia's African-American population.

Lucretia, along with fellow abolitionist Maria Weston Chapman, planned the first Anti-Slavery Convention of American Women, which took place in New York City in May of 1837. Under Lucretia's leadership, female delegates discussed creating petitions to end slavery and proposed publishing writings related to abolition.

Progress over Etiquette

At the first Anti-Slavery Convention of American Women, Lucretia and other delegates made arrangements to publish pamphlets written by Angelina and Sarah Grimké. The sisters were the subject of much debate because of their antislavery speeches to "promiscuous audiences," which featured both men and women. For a female lecturer to address a male audience was quite scandalous in the early 1800s. Lucretia, however, was never one to emphasize etiquette over spreading the message of abolition and viewed the Grimkés' work as social progress.

Unfortunately, people who favored slavery were becoming increasingly hostile toward the abolitionist movement. They were particularly suspicious of groups and meetings that blurred social boundaries where men and women of different racial backgrounds worked together. Riots, vandalism, and even physical violence were common reactions to this fear.

Lucretia put up a brave front in the midst of this threatening and hostile political climate, but she was exhausted by the constant controversy that swirled around her. She also suffered from a recurring stomach problem called dyspepsia. Even then, Lucretia found few moments to slow down and escape the duties, dangers, and debates that characterized her life.

ENDLESS BATTLES AND NEW BEGINNINGS

As Lucretia took on greater responsibilities in the antislavery movement, an increasing number of people questioned her decisions. Even liberal

Hicksite Quakers asked her to limit the amount of time she spent preaching about abolition during meetings. They argued that a gathering devoted to prayer and peaceful contemplation should not be disturbed with a topic so likely to cause tension.

But it was difficult for Lucretia to remain silent. By 1837, she had been making trips as a Public Friend, or traveling minister, for seven years. She had delivered antislavery sermons all over the country. Lucretia never intended to upset Quaker elders, but she felt that she had as much a duty to social justice as she did to obeying religious authorities.

Lucretia experienced even greater controversy when she started supporting the New England Non-Resistance Society. This society was created in September 1838 by Lucretia's longtime friend and fellow abolitionist, William Lloyd Garrison.

Controversy within the Family

Lucretia's actions sometimes led to controversy within her own family. Her mother was displeased that she entertained African-American guests at her home on Sansom Street. This disapproval saddened Lucretia, but she firmly believed in personally demonstrating the same message of tolerance that she preached. As Lucretia said of her mother in a letter to her sister Martha, "Her principles, and long cherished … prejudices are sadly at war with each other … She would far prefer others acting out our principles than my doing so."[3]

Executive Committee of the Pennsylvania Anti-Slavery Society

The society was based on the principle of absolute peace. Nonresistants believed that physical force should rarely be used, regardless of whether the situation involved a person's home, work, or even the defense of his or her country. Several nonresistants refused to support the U.S. government as long as it used force. Many people, including Quakers, regarded Garrison and his new society as radical. They questioned how Lucretia could support such an organization.

In the late 1830s, antislavery advocates began arguing over the "woman question." Some abolitionist groups favored men and women working together. But many people opposed both genders working side by side. Some did not support the idea of equality for women. Some who did support equality still felt that women working directly with men would distract people from the purpose behind the antislavery effort. After all, the goal of abolition was to free African Americans—not to make sure women had the same rights and roles as men.

Garrison fought in favor of female abolitionists and saw to it that Lucretia and other women were elected to the National Executive Committee of the American Anti-Slavery Society in 1840. Abolitionists who disagreed with Garrison's decision formed their own group that only allowed male membership. Despite her disappointment with the split, Lucretia took her place with the committee.

"Am I Not a Woman and a Sister?"

In the 1800s, people often used wax and a stamp called a seal to make an impression on paper that let others know that a document was official or authentic. Most abolitionists worked with a seal that showed a male slave kneeling and saying, "Am I not a man and a brother?"[4] Lucretia was not quick to forget the oppression that women in general—faced. Her seal therefore cleverly included an image of a female slave kneeling and questioning, "Am I not a woman and a sister?"[5]

Though Lucretia unsuccessfully attempted to create peace between members on either side of the "woman question," she realized that the rights of her gender and African Americans were not unrelated. Better conditions for one group would probably lead to improved conditions for the other. As she noted,

> All these subjects of reform are kindred in their nature, and giving to each the proper consideration, will tend to strengthen and nerve the mind for all. … We will not love the slave the less, in loving universal humanity more.[6]

Now that Lucretia had been granted a unique opportunity with the American Anti-Slavery Society, she was determined to make the most of it. For every person who criticized her or tried to keep her quiet, there was another who respected her wisdom and sought her representation. It was these individuals who asked Lucretia and James to serve as delegates to the first World's Anti-Slavery Convention in London, England, in May 1840.

FOURTH OF JULY
'Proclaim Liberty to All.'

THE MASSACHUSETTS ANTI-SLAVERY SOCIETY,

Hereby invite all Friends of Freedom, to a

MASS MEETING,

IN THE BEAUTIFUL AND COMMODIOUS

GROVE AT FRAMINGHAM,

On the Ensuing 4th of July.

To consecrate the day to the cause of Impartial and Universal Liberty, by striking a mortal blow at the existence of Slavery in our Land ; and to which all who "despise fraud, and loathe rapine, and abhor blood," and who "reject with indignation the wild and guilty fantasy that man can hold property in man," are cordially invited. In view of the impious claims and alarming strides of the Slave Power, and of the necessity of combined Northern opposition to it, root and branch, to the utter forgetfulness of all sectarian divisions and party lines—it is hoped and believed that this gathering will be unprecedentedly large, and animated by a spirit equal to the crisis.

ELOQUENT ADDRESSES from the ablest Anti-Slavery Speakers, with **SONGS**, and such **RECREATION** as the beautiful spot invites and furnishes, will occupy the day. Among the Speakers expected, are

WM. L. GARRISON, WENDELL PHILLIPS,
T. W. HIGGINSON, PARKER PILLSBURY,
WM. W. BROWN, C. L. REMOND, A. T. FOSS, S. S. FOSTER, &c.

SPECIAL TRAINS of Cars, for the GROVE, will leave

BOSTON, WORCESTER, MILFORD, and NORTHBORO

At 9 o'clock, A. M., Stopping at Way Stations. Leave MILLBURY at 8 1-2 o'clock, A. M.

FARES AS FOLLOWS:

BOSTON TO THE GROVE AND BACK,		**Sixty Cents for Adults.**
WORCESTER, " " "		**Thirty Cents for Children.**
MILLBURY, " " "		

Milford to the Grove and Back, and Northboro' to the Grove and back, **50 Cents for Adults.**
All Way Stations, on Main Road and Branches, " " " **25 Cents for Children.**

Returning, leave the Grove from 5 to 6 o'clock, P. M.

The HOUSE AT THE GROVE WILL BE OPEN FOR REFRESHMENTS.

☞ In Case of RAIN, the Speaking will be in WAVERLEY HALL, opp. the R. R. Depot at S. Framingham.

Press of Henry J. Howland, 245 Main Street, Worcester.

An abolitionist poster

London, England, in the mid–1800s

THE LEADERSHIP
OF A LIONESS

On May 27, 1840, the Motts arrived in Great Britain for the first World's Anti-Slavery Convention. They were greeted with a mixture of scandal and controversy to which they had become so accustomed. Much of the British Quaker

community—which was largely
Orthodox—regarded them with
suspicion because they were Hicksites.
Other delegates pleaded with Lucretia
to not attend the meeting, or at
least to leave the focus on abolition
rather than on gender equality.
They reminded her that the "woman
question" was not of much debate
in Great Britain. British female
abolitionists had their own societies
and had no intention of pushing for
a presence at the convention.

Once the gathering officially
began on June 12, the male delegates
voted that female abolitionists
should not play an active role in the
proceedings. Those women who
wished to stay should sit in the back of
the hall. From this section, Lucretia
watched the convention in silence
with fellow abolitionist Elizabeth
Cady Stanton. While Lucretia may
not have realized it at the time, her
introduction to Stanton marked

Poverty Next to Palaces

The Motts spent about three months in Europe, touring several British cities. Lucretia noted that social injustices did not merely exist on American soil. The Motts observed that laborers lived in stark poverty not far from luxurious and sprawling estates. James later wrote a short book detailing the highlights of their trip. He described Windsor Palace as "one of the many monuments to the extravagance and folly of the British nobility and aristocracy, which oppressed the laborer, taking from him in the shape of … taxes so much of his earnings as to leave but a scarce subsistence for himself."[1]

the start of a long-lasting friendship and a dynamic partnership in the fight for women's rights.

Driven to be heard on some level, Lucretia was finally allowed to address the audience at a follow-up meeting the next day. Some men attempted to silence her as she discussed the topic of free produce. But an even greater number wanted to hear her voice and expressed their encouragement. Though Lucretia wished she could have contributed more, she returned to Philadelphia a changed person.

Sitting in Silence

Lucretia considered it somewhat ridiculous that the 1840 convention in London included the word *World's* in its title, as the meeting was clearly not open to all of the world's citizens. As frustrating as her exclusion was, she still decided to remain present in Freemason's Hall and witness the gathering from afar. Before the proceedings drew to a close, Lucretia and other female abolitionists privately voiced their displeasure to male delegates who preferred that they sit in silence. These women insisted that their oppressors did a disservice not only to women, but also to slaves and the abolitionist movement in general.

Describing her observations in a letter to fellow abolitionist Maria Weston Chapman, she noted,

> ...the name "The World's Convention" was merely a "poetical license"—a rhetorical flourish ... Of course we would not thrust ourselves forward into such a meeting, but having come so far to see what could be done for the Slave, and being thus prevented doing anything ourselves, we were willing to be mere lookers on and listeners ... from without. We had many opportunities ... to present to [male delegates] their injustice to us—to the cause of the slave —as well as their own inconsistency.[2]

She may have said little to the formal assembly, but her mere presence was powerful enough to have earned her the nickname the "lioness of the convention."[3]

London made Lucretia as devoted as ever to abolition, but it also caused her to discover a renewed dedication to women's rights. She and Stanton had talked about organizing a group in the United States that would focus on that cause. The experience of being oppressed emboldened Lucretia. She was ready to pour forth completely her emotions, passions, and talents into the causes she held dear—regardless of who might try to get in her way.

A Spirited Traveler and a Significant Tea Party

Between 1840 and 1844, Lucretia resumed her public ministry with a new sense of freedom and determination. It was expected that everyone from Quaker elders to pro-slavery mobs would lash out against her. But Lucretia had a clear focus on all the people she could help—rather than the handful who opposed her. She and James traveled throughout the eastern, midwestern, and southern United

President John Tyler

States, speaking out against slavery. Their argument
for abolition often was met with cold silence or
outright hostility—especially in areas that allowed
slavery. It was not easy for the Motts to keep their

spirits up when innkeepers refused to house them or when their carriage was vandalized. Even some Quakers sought to disown Lucretia for her continued outspokenness on the subject of slavery.

Despite these frustrations, there were also a sufficient number of rewarding moments during which her message fell on prominent and powerful ears. Lucretia visited the nation's capital in early 1843, and had a private audience with President John Tyler. She also addressed more than 40 U.S. congressmen and caught the attention and admiration of poet Ralph Waldo Emerson. As Emerson said of one audience's reaction to her preaching, "It was like the rumble of an earthquake—the sensation that attended the speech."[4]

Unfortunately, personal tragedy temporarily halted Lucretia's travel agenda. In the spring of 1844, she and her mother became sick with

President John Tyler

President John Tyler was a slave owner and the last president in favor of slave labor. He defended the states' rights to own slaves. He also favored the idea of establishing a settlement in West Africa where freed slaves would be sent to live. Lucretia strongly opposed this philosophy and argued that African Americans should enjoy the same rights and privileges due any citizen. "He professed some interest in the subject [of slavery] but thought the blacks should be colonized," she later explained in a letter. "He asked if we would be willing to have them at the North. I replied, 'Yes—as many as incline to come.'"[5]

influenza. On March 26, her 73-year-old mother died. Lucretia recovered but was crushed by the loss of her remaining parent. She was also physically weakened from her own illness. For the next three years, she directed much of her attention to local social reform. She developed organizations and promoted efforts that helped Philadelphia's poor. She also gave her first sermons on women's rights—a mere hint of the crusade she would wage in the years to come.

When she finally began traveling again in the spring of 1847, Lucretia preached about the antislavery movement to crowds that sometimes numbered in the thousands. But by the summer of 1848, she unknowingly set forth on a path that would make a permanent mark on women's rights. That July, Lucretia met with her sister Martha and Elizabeth Cady Stanton in New York. Also present were Hicksite acquaintances Mary Ann McClintock and Jane Hunt.

Over tea, the five women discussed their lots in life. Though they valued their roles as wives and mothers, they were frustrated and depressed by the

"...like the slave, [woman] is pressed down by laws in the making of which she has no voice, and crushed by customs that have grown out of such laws. She cannot rise therefore, while thus trampled in the dust. The oppressor does not see himself in that light until the oppressed cry for deliverance."[6]

–Lucretia Mott

Fellow women's rights advocate and co-organizer of the Seneca Falls Convention, Mary Ann McClintock

routine of household chores and responsibilities. Like so many other women, they were intelligent and capable—but the greater opportunities in universities, various professions, and politics were denied to them. The quintet decided to place an official announcement in the local newspaper.

The Self-evident Truths of Seneca Falls

The *Seneca County Courier* ran their announcement of a convention "to discuss the social, civil, and religious conditions and rights of woman." The meeting was scheduled for July 19 to July 20, 1848, at Wesleyan Chapel in Seneca Falls, New York. Lucretia and other organizers initially planned for the gathering to be open only to women on July 19. But in the end, they allowed men to be present when a massive mixed crowd flooded inside the chapel.

The event was more popular than the five women anticipated. Those in attendance listened to them speak about the current social status of women and the need to improve their opportunities and rights. Like many other conventions of the day, the first Women's Rights Convention featured a Declaration of Sentiments. It was strikingly similar to the Declaration

Practicality in Reality

Leaders at Seneca Falls were aware of the struggles they faced. They also realized the Declaration of Sentiments needed a practical tone and realistic goals. Accordingly, text included the following passage: "In entering upon the great work before us, we anticipate no small amount of misconception, misrepresentation, and ridicule; but we shall use every instrumentality within our power to effect our object. We shall employ agents, circulate tracts, petition the State and national Legislatures, and endeavor to enlist the pulpit and the press in our behalf. We hope this Convention will be followed by a series of conventions, embracing every part of the country."[7]

An illustration of the first Women's Rights Convention

of Independence but featured wording specific
to women and the goals of the meeting. The text
opened with the powerful assertion, "We hold these
truths to be self-evident: that *all men and women* are
created equal ..."[8]

Organizers proposed several resolutions that
called for equal treatment of both genders. Leaders
at the convention wanted the government to repeal
legislation that was against these resolutions. They
wanted men and women to be held to the same
moral standards. They also wanted to make it more

socially acceptable for women to speak publicly to mixed-gender audiences and to pursue careers in professions outside the home. Perhaps the most controversial was the resolution that called for women to fight for suffrage—the right to vote.

As the convention concluded, all of these resolutions were adopted. One hundred of the people in attendance—both male and female— proudly signed the Declaration of Sentiments. Like most major steps in social reform, the Seneca Falls Convention provoked mixed reactions that included praise, ridicule, and a fear of change. Regardless of whether she was being criticized or admired, Lucretia's name again captured the attention of friends, enemies, and people hoping for the progress she demanded. ⌐

An engraving of Elizabeth Cady Stanton speaking at the first Women's Rights Convention in Seneca Falls, New York

*Susan B. Anthony and Elizabeth Cady Stanton,
women's rights leaders and friends of Lucretia Mott*

SOCIAL STRIDES AND A
COSTLY CONFLICT

Less than two weeks after the success at
Seneca Falls, Lucretia was speaking at a
second Women's Rights Convention in Rochester,
New York. This time, the audience tested her
knowledge of the Bible and of Holy Scripture.

A few attendees noted that certain biblical passages suggested men should rule over women. Surely Lucretia, a Quaker minister, would never recommend that the public disregard the Bible in favor of controversial social reform. Quick-minded and just as knowledgeable about Holy Scripture, Lucretia countered each of their arguments. She observed that Saint Paul also advised men not to marry. Clearly, it was necessary to apply reason when interpreting religious writings.

The Rochester convention was not the last time that women's rights opponents would quote scripture to try to further their cause. In the autumn of 1849, writer Richard Henry Dana Sr. arrived in Philadelphia to lecture. His speech, "An Address on Woman," referenced both classic literature and the Bible as examples of why the concept of equal rights for women was ridiculous, as well as socially dangerous. The world was eager to see if Lucretia would formally respond to his lecture. She did not disappoint them.

On December 17, 1849, she issued her own formal speech, "Discourse on Woman." Lucretia mentioned biblical examples ranging from the Garden of Eden to the teachings of Christ to demonstrate how formal religion could also be used to support women's rights. She passionately expressed that equality was not a special favor—it was what women deserved and were entitled to. Women could make vast contributions to both academics and countless professions if society would only acknowledge their right to do so. As she explained,

> The question is often asked, "What does woman want, more than she enjoys? What is she seeking to obtain? Of what rights is she deprived? What privileges are with-

On the Subject of Marriage

Lucretia shared a strong relationship with James that was rooted in mutual respect as each regarded the other as an equal. In contrast, she witnessed how some women's husbands, who legally controlled their money and personal property, expected their wives to submit to their will and opinions. Lucretia recognized a need for a change in laws and overall attitudes. In her speech, "Discourse on Woman," Lucretia stated,

> The law of husband and wife, as you gather it from the books, is a disgrace to any civilized nation. ... The legal theory is, that marriage makes the husband and wife one person, and that person is the husband. ... There is no foundation in reason or expediency, for the absolute and slavish subjection of the wife to the husband, which forms the foundation of the present legal relations. Were woman, in point of fact, the abject thing which the law, in theory, considers her to be when married, she would not be worthy the companionship of man. I would ask if such a code of laws does not require change? If such a condition of the wife in society does not claim redress? On no good ground can reform be delayed.[1]

held from her?" I answer, she asks nothing as favor, but as right, she wants to be acknowledged a moral, responsible being.[2]

A MUCH SOUGHT-AFTER INFLUENCE

Lucretia's words had a far-reaching impact. Not only was her speech published as a pamphlet, but she also became more sought after as an advocate of women's rights. She continued corresponding with Elizabeth Cady Stanton and inspired younger reformers such as Lucy Stone and Susan B. Anthony to take an active part in the crusade for gender equality. Additionally, Lucretia helped raise money for schools that provided enhanced educational opportunities for women to pursue professional careers in everything from medicine to art.

Despite this extremely full schedule, Lucretia maintained a busy personal life. In 1851, the Motts moved to an even more massive house

Are Women Superior?

A few supporters of the women's rights movement asserted the belief that women were not just equal to men—they were superior. Lucretia rejected this philosophy. Speaking at the fourth National Women's Rights Convention in 1854, she expressed her reasoning, "We ought … to claim no more for woman than for man; we ought to put woman on a par with man, not invest her with power, or claim her superiority over her brother. If we do, she is just as likely to become a tyrant as man is … It is always unsafe to invest man with power over his fellow being. 'Call no man master'—that is a true doctrine."[3]

The Temperance Movement

In addition to advocating abolition and gender equality, Lucretia was also a strong supporter of temperance—a movement that encouraged people to drink alcoholic beverages in moderation or avoid them altogether. Many social reformers believed that alcohol use led to unnecessary violence and domestic abuse. Temperance was particularly appealing to nonresistants and women's rights leaders such as Lucretia. As she proudly exclaimed during a speech in 1860, "The temperance reformation has accomplished almost a revolution in our age."[4]

on Arch Street that also became home to several of their children and grandchildren. Lucretia continued to receive numerous requests to preside over or attend women's rights conventions, which had been held on a national level starting in 1850. She was eager to lend her support and to offer her thoughts and ideas, but she also hoped that younger reformers would assume a more dominant role in the women's rights movement.

By the time Lucretia led the third National Women's Rights Convention in Syracuse, New York, in 1852, she was 59 years old. That meeting—as well as another equal rights gathering held in New York City the following year—was filled with loud and cruel objections from women's rights opponents. Already familiar with angry mobs that did not share her views, she rallied the women to have courage and consistently saw to their safety.

Lucretia was becoming increasingly eager to hand over leadership to the next generation of female reformers. They realized, as perhaps Lucretia secretly did, that she was the backbone that helped the movement withstand such hostile opposition. Regardless of her prominent role in women's rights, she did not forsake her work in abolition. The cause of freedom was more critical than ever, especially with the nation on the verge of erupting into a bloody conflict over slavery.

The High Price of Freedom

As time passed and politicians from the North and South continued to argue about slavery, African Americans were becoming more desperate for liberty. Though it was a risky decision, many attempted to flee to the free states in the North or to Canada through the Underground Railroad. The Underground Railroad was a network of abolitionists who helped hide escaped slaves on their journey from the South to the North. The danger of their journey was real. If fugitive slaves were caught, they would likely be returned to their masters in the South, who had the right to beat or kill them for their disloyalty.

A staunch believer in the cause, Lucretia welcomed runaways to use her home as a refuge. Under the Fugitive Slave Act of 1850, she and James faced harsh penalties if they were discovered, including a $1,000 fine and half a year in prison. Lucretia remained undaunted, but she also longed for the day when slavery would be completely abolished and African Americans would no longer have to make their dangerous trip to the free states in the North. That day was not far off.

A Welcoming Home

A variety of people made stops at the Motts' home on Arch Street, ranging from prestigious social reformers to poverty-stricken African Americans begging for money. No matter who knocked on her door, Lucretia always attempted to be as hospitable and generous as possible. As James wrote of her, "Lucretia has numerous calls almost daily from all sorts of folks, high and low, rich and poor, for respect, advice, assistance, etc., etc. ... it seems as though some people thought she could do anything and everything."[5]

In March 1857, the Motts moved north of Philadelphia to a farmhouse in the countryside of Chelten Hills, Pennsylvania. By that time, James had been retired for six years, but he and Lucretia remained active in social reform.

James and Lucretia celebrated their jubilant fiftieth wedding anniversary in April 1861. That month also marked the first shots fired in the Civil War. Southern states began to break away from the U.S. government to form the Confederacy. Citizens loyal to

Banner of the Third U.S. Colored Troop,
an African-American regiment fighting in the Civil War

President Lincoln and the concept of preserving the
nation supported the Union forces.

Roadside, as the Motts called their Chelten
Hills farmhouse, was located next to Camp William
Penn. Union troops used the farmland to train
African-American recruits. Lucretia frequently sent

fresh fruits, vegetables, and homemade treats to the young men. She even spoke at the camp, comforting soldiers by reminding them that one day they would be living in peace.

It was difficult to remember these words during years of conflict that left approximately 600,000 troops lying dead by the war's end. The conflict

The Race Street Sewing Society

Lucretia realized that life would not be easy for slaves emancipated during the Civil War. Their liberty did not end discrimination. As the conflict continued, she raised money and sewed blankets and clothes for the freed slaves. She also created a group at the Race Street Meeting in Philadelphia that performed similar work. In January 1864, she proudly wrote, "We are really beginning to *do something*. The Race Street Sewing Society have made up and forwarded 7,000 garments—as many thousand dollars have been placed at their disposal."[6]

posed complicated questions for Lucretia, who was both a Quaker and a nonresistant. As an abolitionist, she wanted to see an end to slavery, but at what cost? Even when the Civil War ended in 1865 and slavery was declared unconstitutional, she had a difficult time acknowledging that the bloodshed had been justified. Lucretia was now 72 years old and still perceived the need for a more decent society that would stamp out every variety of discrimination in a peaceful manner.

In pursuance of the sixth section of the act of Congress entitled "An act to suppress insurrection and to punish treason and rebellion, to seize and confiscate property of rebels, and for other purposes" Approved July 17. 1862, and which act, and the Joint Resolution explanatory thereof, are herewith published, I, Abraham Lincoln, President of the United States, do hereby proclaim to, and warn all persons within the contemplation of said sixth section to cease participating in, aiding, countenancing, or abetting the existing rebellion, or any rebellion against the government of the United States, and to return to their proper allegiance to the United States, on pain of the forfeitures and seizures, as within and by said sixth section provided—

And I hereby make known that it is my purpose, upon the next meeting of Congress, to again recommend the adoption of a practical measure for tendering pecuniary aid to the free choice or rejection, of any and all States which may then be recognizing and practically sustaining the authority of the United States, and which may then have voluntarily adopted, or thereafter may voluntarily adopt, gradual abolishment ~~adoption~~ of slavery, within such State or States— that the object is to practically restore, thenceforward to be maintain, the constitutional relation between the general government, and each, and all the states, wherein that relation

African-American men voting for the first time

Peace, Loss, and an Ageless Legacy

ucretia was not surprised to witness that the world was less than perfect after the Civil War. She and James lent their wholehearted support to efforts that helped African Americans receive equal treatment. They joined groups such as the Friends' Association of Philadelphia for the Aid and Elevation of the Freedmen. Quakers created the organization in 1865 to provide African Americans with improved schooling and to fight for laws that would help eliminate discrimination.

Lucretia and James worked one-on-one with Philadelphia's African-American community. They helped raise money for orphanages and prepared baked goods for a local African-American nursing home. Though slaves had been freed, they still did not have many job or educational opportunities. Until the passage of the Fifteenth Amendment in 1870, African-American men—just like women of any race—did not have the right to vote. Discrimination created poverty, frustration, and violence.

Along with her continued aid to the African-American community, the Civil War had also further committed Lucretia to the cause of peace. Both she and James played a role in founding the Pennsylvania Peace Society in 1866. This society encouraged people to resolve problems without violence by relying on intelligence and a sense of morality. Lucretia also agreed to act as president of the American Equal Rights Association. Established in 1866, this association shared her belief that the causes of women and African Americans were undeniably intertwined. The organization was concerned with promoting the rights of both groups and of "all American citizens ... irrespective of race, color, or sex."[1]

The Fourteenth Amendment, which touched on the issue of voting rights, was about to put the unity within several reform movements to the test. The wording of the amendment only addressed voting privileges for "male citizens."[2] African-American *men* were referenced in this

---

Though the Chains Have Been Melted

After the Civil War, even whites in northern states frequently did not want African Americans as their neighbors and generally preferred not to share the same schools or public facilities with them. Segregation was rampant, and Lucretia was determined to prove the stupidity of this social injustice. As she observed in preparation for the first anniversary of the American Equal Rights Association in 1867,

> The black man is still denied the crowning right of citizenship ... though the fires of civil war have melted the chains ... and a hundred battlefields attest his courage and patriotism.[3]

When Camp William Penn in Pennsylvania closed in 1865, Lucretia strongly advocated that the land be used to create a mixed racial community, which was ultimately named La Mott in her honor. Lucretia also campaigned for African Americans to be allowed to ride in Philadelphia's horse-drawn streetcars—a privilege that they were not fully allowed until the twentieth century. For Lucretia, it was essential to make liberty a reality for African Americans in every sense of the word.

phrase, but there was no mention of women of any race.

Some women's rights advocates were only slightly troubled by the wording. They preferred to lobby for legislation that would improve their gender's career and educational opportunities. But several reformers were aghast at the slight. Supporters of the amendment pointed to the fact that at least African-American men might possibly have a voice in national affairs. In their opinion, gender equality also deserved consideration, but African Americans desperately needed the opportunity to vote. They lived in a severely unfair and often dangerous world where whites sometimes used violence to express racial hatred and discrimination. Could women claim the same?

Lucretia attempted to calm both sides of the argument, but tensions ultimately grew deeper.

A Humble Woman

Lucretia frequently proved to be the subject of great controversy. She also was tremendously popular and respected toward the end of her life. She was besieged with letters. People asked for her autograph and named their daughters and various reform groups in her honor. Always modest and more concerned with promoting social causes than personal fame, Lucretia once noted, "I'm much an over-rated woman, it's humiliating."[4]

The fight for women's suffrage continued for many decades until 1920, when women were finally given the right to vote.

She continued to attend various conventions and even led the American Equal Rights Association's yearly meeting in 1867. The debate surrounding the amendment affected her. She was tired, frustrated, and susceptible to stomach problems. These complaints, however, would soon be replaced by an overwhelming sense of loss and the end of a 56-year marriage.

MOURNING AND MOVING FORWARD

January 1868 was a bleak month for Lucretia. Neither she nor James was in the best of health.

They were staying with their daughter Pattie in New York to attend a wedding. James was diagnosed with pneumonia and was too sick to return to Roadside. He died on January 26. Lucretia traveled to Philadelphia to bury her husband. The Quaker community did its best to comfort her.

Lucretia had long ceased to be the center of controversy within most Quaker circles. She still did not have their complete approval, but they were aware of how society was undertaking the changes she had championed for so many years. Members of her religion and other Philadelphians expressed their regret at the passing of Lucretia's husband and her personal loss.

The topic of suffrage helped take her mind off James's death. The Fourteenth Amendment was ratified, or approved, in 1868. This amendment stated that all persons

The Perfect Establishment

In the 1860s, Lucretia, James, and other Hicksites made plans to open a boarding school called Swarthmore College near Philadelphia. The Motts were adamant that the school be coeducational and played a major role in its development. James was also a member of the board of managers.

After her husband's death, Lucretia acted as an advisor to the board and attended opening ceremonies in October 1869. Proud of her husband's contributions to education, she gave the school two oak trees that James had originally planted at Roadside. As she noted of Swarthmore's inauguration day, "…all the scholars seemed perfectly happy—and well they may be—for 'tis a perfect Establishment."[5]

Fifteenth Amendment

Section 1. "The right of citizens of the United States to vote shall not be denied or abridged by the United States or by any state on account of race, color, or previous condi- tion of servitude." Ratified on February 3, 1870, the Fifteenth Amendment of- ficially gave all African- American male citizens the right to vote. Another 50 years would have to pass until women could claim the same right.[6]

born within the United States were considered citizens of the United States, including former slaves. This amendment also touched on the right to vote, stating that male citizens 21 years of age and older had voting rights. However, many argued that this did not explicitly grant the right to African Americans.

However, legislators did seem in favor of the Fifteenth Amendment, which was proposed in 1869. The Fifteenth Amendment explicitly guaranteed African-American men the right to vote, but women were again dismissed. While Lucretia ultimately supported women's suffrage, she did her best to reconcile the various factions that were forming in response to the amendments.

Lucretia also continued to advocate peace, especially upon being elected president of the Pennsylvania Peace Society in 1870. In this role, she passionately opposed

The Motts' farmhouse, Roadside

military training in public schools, as well as capital punishment. She frequently spoke out for Native Americans facing government execution because they resisted moving to reservations and giving up their land.

In addition to attending conventions, Lucretia often preached at the Race Street Meeting and attempted to answer the endless stream of letters that arrived at Roadside. Unfortunately, old age and recurring stomach problems posed an increasing challenge to her countless commitments. The white–

haired and somewhat frail social reformer turned 83 in 1876—the same year America celebrated 100 years of history, change, and progress.

A Prophesy of the Future of Woman

Though Lucretia's family was concerned that she continued to travel so much, she remained independent and determined. She made a final trip to Nantucket Island in 1876 and was present at the thirtieth anniversary of the Seneca Falls Convention in New York in 1878. When she was no longer able to venture out of state, she traveled to Philadelphia for local gatherings related to peace and equal rights. By 1879, however, even these meetings proved too exhausting. By autumn of that year, she rarely left her bed at Roadside.

Lucretia had outlived many of her relatives— including three of her children and several grandchildren. Lucretia's surviving family members

The Nineteenth Amendment

"The right of citizens of the United States to vote shall not be denied or abridged by the United States or by any state on account of sex."[7] The Nineteenth Amendment to the U.S. Constitution was ratified on August 18, 1920. The amendment finally granted American women suffrage nearly 40 years after Lucretia's death.

met at the farmhouse and tried to make her as comfortable as possible. She died on November 11, 1880, at the age of 87. A crowd of thousands gathered to witness her burial next to James at the Fair Hill Burial Grounds in north Philadelphia. Several subsequent memorial services were arranged across the nation by the organizations and people that held her dear. Just as she had made newspaper headlines during her life for the bold and uncompromising attitude she took toward social reform, numerous publications now reported her passing and recounted her many accomplishments.

What may have pleased Lucretia more than these tributes, however, was a letter she received shortly before her death. Lucy Stone wrote and told Lucretia how she had been remembered in a resolution at the thirtieth anniversary of the first National Women's Rights Convention:

> *Resolved, that this convention presents its greetings to its venerable early leader and friend, Lucretia Mott, whose life in its rounded perfection as wife, mother, preacher, and reformer is the prophesy of the future of woman. ... We think of you, dear Mrs. Mott, with loving tenderness and sympathy in your feeble health, but we remember the other days of*

strength, and the help given so freely to our inexperience, in the sure belief that the good cause we have sought to establish will surely be carried at no distant day. [8]

Stone's note offered Lucretia what she would have desired most—the promise that future generations would continue promoting the social progress that she preached about, made sacrifices for, and was dedicated to seeing achieved. ⌐

Who Can Speak?

A famous story recounts how there was solemn silence at Lucretia's graveside, though thousands of people were gathered to pay their respects. Finally, someone asked, "Will no one say anything?"[9] Recalling her eloquence and the many meaningful public speeches that characterized her life, another mourner replied, "Who can speak? The preacher is dead."[10]

Lucretia Mott

TIMELINE

1793	1808	1811
Lucretia is born to Thomas Coffin Jr. and Anna Folger Coffin on January 3.	Lucretia completes the curriculum at Nine Partners and accepts a job as an assistant teacher at the school.	Lucretia marries James Mott on April 10.

1827	1830	1833
Lucretia begins attending Cherry Street Meeting and formally demonstrates her allegiance to Hicksites.	Lucretia begins an active ministry as a Public Friend, preaching throughout the United States.	Lucretia begins to suffer from stomach problems known as dyspepsia.

1817

Lucretia's son Tommy dies from a fever in April.

1821

Lucretia is formally recognized as a Quaker minister in January.

Mid-1820s

At home, the Motts begin a boycott on goods produced through slave labor.

1833

On December 5, Lucretia attends a convention in Philadelphia dedicated to the formation of the American Anti-Slavery Society.

1833

On December 9, Lucretia meets with 30 other women to discuss forming the Philadelphia Female Anti-Slavery Society.

1837

Lucretia is organizer and speaker at the first Anti-Slavery Convention of American Women May 9–20.

TIMELINE

1838	1840	1843
On May 17, Pennsylvania Hall is burned down by a mob rioting against the second Anti-Slavery Convention of American Women.	James and Lucretia attend the World's Anti-Slavery Convention in England on June 12.	In January, Lucretia speaks in Washington, D.C., to President John Tyler, 40 congressmen, and poet Ralph Waldo Emerson.

1861	1863	1866
In April, the Civil War begins.	On July 12, Lucretia speaks to African-American troops at Camp William Penn, which is located next to Roadside.	Lucretia and James help found the Pennsylvania Peace Society in January.

1848

On July 19–20, Lucretia leads the first Women's Rights Convention. One hundred delegates sign a Declaration of Sentiments.

1848

In August, Lucretia speaks about women's rights in New York; she addresses questions concerning women's rights and Holy Scripture.

1849

Lucretia delivers her speech, "Discourse on Woman," in Philadelphia on December 17.

1868

James Mott dies of pneumonia in New York on January 26.

1869

On February 26, the Fifteenth Amendment is proposed, addressing the voting rights of African-American males but not of women.

1880

On November 11, Lucretia dies at Roadside at the age of 87.

ESSENTIAL FACTS

DATE OF BIRTH

January 3, 1793

PLACE OF BIRTH

Nantucket Island, near Cape Cod, Massachusetts

DATE OF DEATH

November 11, 1880

PARENTS

Thomas Coffin Jr. and Anna Folger Coffin

EDUCATION

Nine Partners boarding school, Dutchess County, New York

MARRIAGE

James Mott, April 10, 1811

CHILDREN

Anna, Thomas ("Tommy"), Maria, Thomas, Elizabeth, and Martha ("Pattie")

RESIDENCES

Nantucket Island; Boston, Massachusetts; Dutchess County, New York; Philadelphia, Pennsylvania; Mamaroneck, New York; Chelten Hills, Pennsylvania

CAREER HIGHLIGHTS

❖ In 1821, Lucretia was formally recognized as a Quaker minister and began actively preaching her ideals of equality and faith.

❖ In 1837, Lucretia acted as organizer and speaker of the first Anti-Slavery Convention of American Women.

❖ In 1848, Lucretia presided over the first Women's Rights Convention.

❖ In 1849, Lucretia delivered her famous speech, "Discourse on Woman," in Philadelphia.

SOCIETAL CONTRIBUTION

Throughout her life, Lucretia Mott was an active social reformer and Quaker minister. She dedicated her life to the abolition of slavery, the advancement of women's rights, and the concepts of nonresistance and equality.

CONFLICTS

In late 1827, the Quaker community was divided into two groups and Lucretia allied herself with the more liberal "Hicksites," causing a split from many friends and family who were Orthodox members.

Throughout her life, Lucretia also experienced criticism, vandalism, harassment, and even the threat of disownment for promoting the social causes that she supported.

QUOTE

"I have no idea of submitting tamely to injustice ... I will oppose it with all the moral powers with which I am endowed. I am no advocate of passivity." —*Lucretia Mott*

ADDITIONAL RESOURCES

SELECT BIBLIOGRAPHY

Bacon, Margaret Hope, ed. *Lucretia Mott Speaking: Excerpts from the Sermons and Speeches of a Famous Nineteenth-Century Quaker Minister and Reformer*. Wallingford, PA: Pendle Hill Publications, 1980.

Bacon, Margaret H. *Valiant Friend: The Life of Lucretia Mott*. New York: Walker and Company, 1980.

Palmer, Beverly Wilson, ed. *Selected Letters of Lucretia Coffin Mott*. Urbana and Chicago: University of Illinois Press, 2002.

Roslewicz, Elizabeth A. "Educating Adults through Distinctive Public Speaking: Lucretia Mott, Quaker Minister." Diss. Virginia Tech., 1999. Virginia Tech.: Digital Library and Archives. <http://scholar.lib.vt.edu/theses/available/etd-042199-022852/unrestricted>.

The Lucretia Coffin Mott Papers Project. Ed. Beverly Wilson Palmer. Mar. 1998. Pomona College. <http://www.mott.pomona.edu>.

FURTHER READING

Bryant, Jennifer. *Lucretia Mott: A Guiding Light*. Grand Rapids, MI: W. B. Eerdmans Publishing Company, 1996.

Davis, Lucile. *Lucretia Mott: A Photo-Illustrated Biography*. Mankato, MN: Bridgestone Books, 1998.

DeAngelis, Gina. *Lucretia Mott: Woman Suffragist*. Philadelphia: Chelsea House Publishers, 2001.

Kops, Deborah. *Women's Suffrage*. San Diego: Blackbirch Press, 2004.

Web Links

To learn more about Lucretia Mott, visit ABDO Publishing
Company on the World Wide Web at **www.abdopublishing.com**.
Web sites about Lucretia Mott are featured on our Book Links page.
These links are routinely monitored and updated to provide the
most current information available.

Places To Visit

**The Civil War and Underground Railroad Museum
of Philadelphia**
1805 Pine Street, Philadelphia, PA 19103
215-735-8196
www.cwurmuseum.org
This museum features thousands of photographs, artifacts,
weapons, and artwork related to the Civil War and Underground
Railroad.

Friends Historical Library at Swarthmore College
500 College Avenue, Swarthmore, PA 19081
610-328-8496
www.swarthmore.edu/x6662.xml
The Friends Historical Library features a multitude of collections
where visitors may view letters, photos, and other historical
documents related to the Religious Society of Friends.

National Women's Hall of Fame
76 Fall Street, Seneca Falls, NY 13148
315-568-8060
www.greatwomen.org
At the National Women's Hall of Fame visitors can view exhibits and
artifacts related to great American women. There is also a research
library and office where visitors may learn about women who
contributed to—among other things—the arts, athletics, sciences,
and social causes of the United States.

Glossary

abolitionist
A social reformer who supported ending slavery.

amendment
A change or addition to the U.S. Constitution.

boycott
A form of protest in which citizens refuse to buy certain goods or engage in certain activities.

Confederacy
Southern states that broke away from the U.S. government beginning in 1861.

delegate
A person appointed to act as a representative.

discrimination
Unequal treatment of a person often based on gender, religion, or race.

disownment
To deny connection or membership to someone (often as a means of discipline).

dyspepsia
Digestive problems.

elder
A Quaker who oversees the work of ministers and who guides the spiritual and moral well being of other members of their faith.

emancipate
To free or liberate.

free produce
Goods produced without the use of slave labor.

free state
A state that did not allow slavery.

freedman
A former slave who was freed.

Hicksite
> A liberal Quaker who supported the viewpoints of Elias Hicks; Hicksites believed in less restrictive rules and a stronger focus on the Inward Light than Orthodox Quakers.

Inward Light
> The Quaker notion that all people are illuminated, or guided, by God speaking directly to them or through their consciences.

Monthly Meeting
> A specific group of Quakers who gather based on geographic location to worship and discuss business.

Nonresistance
> A philosophy that rejects individual or government use of force, weapons, or violence for conflict resolution.

Orthodox
> Following a strict set of rules and customs within one's religion. Orthodox Quakers opposed the ideas expressed by Hicksites and relied more heavily on rules and the guidance of elders.

Quaker
> A member of the Religious Society of Friends. Quakers believe in concepts such as simplicity, peace, obedience, and inward reflection.

segregation
> The separation of people based on race, class, ethnicity, gender, or other classifications.

suffrage
> The right to vote.

Underground Railroad
> A system in which abolitionists helped hide African-American slaves as they escaped from slave states to the Northern free states or Canada.

Union
> Northern states that remained loyal to the U.S. government and President Abraham Lincoln during the Civil War.

SOURCE NOTES

1. Making a Statement by Facing the Mob

1. Margaret Hope Bacon. *Valiant Friend: The Life of Lucretia Mott*. New York: Walker and Company, 1980. 5.
2. Ibid. 6.
3. Beverly Wilson Palmer, ed. *Selected Letters of Lucretia Coffin Mott*. Urbana and Chicago: University of Illinois Press, 2002.
4. *Women's Words of Wisdom: Thoughts Over Time*. 4 Feb. 2004. The Library of Congress. 7 Feb. 2007 <http://memory.loc.gov/learn/features/womenswords/alternative.html>.
5. *Lucretia Coffin Mott (1793-1880)*. 29 Nov. 2006. The Future of Freedom Foundation. 8 Feb. 2007 < http://www.fff.org/freedom/fd0608f.asp>.

2. A Taste of Equality on Nantucket Island

1. Margaret Hope Bacon. *Valiant Friend: The Life of Lucretia Mott*. New York: Walker and Company, 1980. 14.
2. *The Spiritual Leadership of George Fox*. 12 Aug. 2004. George Fox University. 3 Mar. 2007 <http://georgefox.edu/about/georgefox/leadership.html>.
3. Beverly Wilson Palmer, ed. *Selected Letters of Lucretia Coffin Mott*. Urbana and Chicago: University of Illinois Press, 2002. 234.
4. Margaret Hope Bacon. *Valiant Friend: The Life of Lucretia Mott*. New York: Walker and Company, 1980. 14.
5. Beverly Wilson Palmer, ed. *Selected Letters of Lucretia Coffin Mott*. Urbana and Chicago: University of Illinois Press, 2002. 142.
6. Elizabeth A. Roslewicz. "Educating Adults through Distinctive Public Speaking: Lucretia Mott, Quaker Minister." Diss. Virginia Tech., 1999. Virginia Tech.: Digital Library and Archives. 3 March 2007 <http://scholar.lib.vt.edu/theses/available/etd-042199-022852/unrestricted/ADDENDUM.PDF>.
7. Margaret Hope Bacon. *Valiant Friend: The Life of Lucretia Mott*. New York: Walker and Company, 1980. 17.

3. A Life-altering Education

1. Margaret Hope Bacon, ed. *Lucretia Mott Speaking: Excerpts from the Sermons & Speeches of a Famous Nineteenth Century Quaker Minister & Reformer*. Wallingford, PA: Pendle Hill Publications, 1980. 18 Feb. 2007. The Religious Society of Friends. 3 Mar. 2007 <http://www.quaker.org/mott/memo-on-self.html>.
2. Elias Hicks. "Observations on the Slavery of the Africans and their Descendants, and on the Use of the Produce of their Labor." Philadelphia: T. Ellwood Chapman, 1861. The Quaker Writings Home Page. 18 Sep. 2007. <http://qhpress.org/quakerpages/qwhp/hickslave.htm>.
3. Margaret Hope Bacon. *Valiant Friend: The Life of Lucretia Mott*. New York: Walker and Company, 1980. 24–25.
4. Margaret Hope Bacon, ed. *Lucretia Mott Speaking: Excerpts from the Sermons &*

Speeches of a Famous Nineteenth Century Quaker Minister & Reformer. Wallingford, PA: Pendle Hill Publications, 1980. 18 Feb. 2007. The Religious Society of Friends. 3 Mar. 2007 <http://www.quaker.org/mott/memo-on-self.html>.

5. Margaret Hope Bacon. *Valiant Friend: The Life of Lucretia Mott*. New York: Walker and Company, 1980. 26.

6. Margaret Hope Bacon, ed. *Lucretia Mott Speaking: Excerpts from the Sermons & Speeches of a Famous Nineteenth Century Quaker Minister & Reformer*. Wallingford, PA: Pendle Hill Publications, 1980. 18 Feb. 2007. The Religious Society of Friends. 5 Mar. 2007 <http://www.quaker.org/mott/memo-on-self.html>.

7. Ibid.

8. Margaret Hope Bacon. *Valiant Friend: The Life of Lucretia Mott*. New York: Walker and Company, 1980. 30.

4. Wife, Mother, Quaker Minister

1. Margaret Hope. *Valiant Friend: The Life of Lucretia Mott*. New York: Walker and Company, 1980. 32.

2. Elizabeth A. Roslewicz. "Educating Adults through Distinctive Public Speaking: Lucretia Mott, Quaker Minister." Diss. Virginia Tech., 1999. Virginia Tech.: Digital Library and Archives. 8 Mar. 2007 <http://scholar.lib.vt.edu/theses/available/etd-042199-022852/unrestricted/chapter3a.pdf >.

3. Margaret Hope Bacon, ed. *Lucretia Mott Speaking: Excerpts from the Sermons & Speeches of a Famous Nineteenth Century Quaker Minister & Reformer*. Wallingford, PA: Pendle Hill Publications, 1980. 18 Feb. 2007. The Religious Society of Friends. 5 Mar. 2007 <http://www.quaker.org/mott/memo-on-self.html>.

4. Beverly Wilson Palmer, ed. *Selected Letters of Lucretia Coffin Mott*. Urbana and Chicago: University of Illinois Press, 2002. 454–455.

5. Margaret Hope Bacon. *Valiant Friend: The Life of Lucretia Mott*. New York: Walker and Company, 1980. 36.

6. Beverly Wilson Palmer, ed. *Selected Letters of Lucretia Coffin Mott*. Urbana and Chicago: University of Illinois Press, 2002. 113.

7. Ibid.

5. Courage amid Controversy

1. Beverly Wilson Palmer, ed. *Selected Letters of Lucretia Coffin Mott*. Urbana and Chicago: University of Illinois Press, 2002. 15.

2. Margaret Hope Bacon. *Valiant Friend: The Life of Lucretia Mott*. New York: Walker and Company, 1980. 41.

3. Margaret Hope Bacon, ed. *Lucretia Mott Speaking: Excerpts from the Sermons and Speeches of a Famous Nineteenth-Century Quaker Minister and Reformer*. Wallingford, PA: Pendle Hill Publications, 1980. 11.

4. Ibid. 12.

5. Ibid. 27.

SOURCE NOTES CONTINUED

6. The Voice of Women in the War for Freedom
1. Margaret Hope Bacon, ed. *Lucretia Mott Speaking: Excerpts from the Sermons and Speeches of a Famous Nineteenth-Century Quaker Minister and Reformer*. Wallingford, PA: Pendle Hill Publications, 1980. 57.
2. Margaret Hope Bacon. *Valiant Friend: The Life of Lucretia Mott*. New York: Walker and Company, 1980. 59.
3. Ibid. 60.
4. *Virtual Exhibitions: To Modern Eyes*. Daughters of the American Revolution. 11 Mar. 2007 <http://www.dar.org/museum/exhibitions.cfm>.
5. Ibid.
6. Margaret Hope Bacon, ed. *Lucretia Mott Speaking: Excerpts from the Sermons and Speeches of a Famous Nineteenth-Century Quaker Minister and Reformer*. Wallingford, PA: Pendle Hill Publications, 1980. 13–14.

7. The Leadership of a Lioness
1. Margaret Hope Bacon. *Valiant Friend: The Life of Lucretia Mott*. New York: Walker and Company, 1980. 88.
2. Beverly Wilson Palmer, ed. *Selected Letters of Lucretia Coffin Mott*. Urbana and Chicago: University of Illinois Press, 2002. 78–79.
3. "Sketches of the Anti-Slavery Convention, No. VIII: Lucretia Mott." Assumption College. 12 Mar. 2007 <http://www.assumption.edu/ahc/abolition/MottDiary.html>.
4. Margaret Hope Bacon. *Valiant Friend: The Life of Lucretia Mott*. New York: Walker and Company, 1980. 105.
5. Beverly Wilson Palmer, ed. *Selected Letters of Lucretia Coffin Mott*. Urbana and Chicago: University of Illinois Press, 2002. 121.
6. Margaret H. Bacon, ed. *Lucretia Mott Speaking: Excerpts from the Sermons & Speeches of a Famous Quaker Minister & Reformer*. Wallingford, PA: Pendle Hill Publications, 1980. 21 Aug. 2007. <http://www.pendlehill.org/resources/files/free%20downloads%20pages/php234.php>.
7. "Declaration of Sentiments and Resolution." *The Elizabeth Cady Stanton and Susan B. Anthony Papers Project*. Aug. 2006. Rutgers: The State University of New Jersey. 12 Mar. 2007 <http://ecssba.rutgers.edu/docs/seneca.html>.
8. Ibid.

8. Social Strides and a Costly Conflict
1. "Lesson Two: Changing Methods and Reforms of the Woman's Suffrage Movement, 1840–1920." *Discourse on Woman*. 26 Sept. 2002. The Library of Congress: The Learning Page. 13 Mar. 2007 <http://memory.loc.gov/learn/lessons/99/suffrage/discourse.html>.
2. Ibid.
3. Margaret Hope Bacon, ed. *Lucretia Mott Speaking: Excerpts from the Sermons and Speeches of a Famous Nineteenth-Century Quaker Minister and Reformer*. Wallingford, PA:

Pendle Hill Publications, 1980. 16.

4. Anna Davis Hallowell, ed. "Righteousness Exalteth a Nation: A Sermon Delivered by Lucretia Mott." 3 June 2004. The Quaker Homiletics Online Anthology, Part Three: The Nineteenth Century. 18 Mar. 2007 <http://www.qhpress.org/quakerpages/qhoa/mott.htm>.

5. Margaret Hope Bacon. *Valiant Friend: The Life of Lucretia Mott.* New York: Walker and Company, 1980. 161.

6. Beverly Wilson Palmer, ed. *Selected Letters of Lucretia Coffin Mott.* Urbana and Chicago: University of Illinois Press, 2002. 338.

9. Peace, Loss, and an Ageless Legacy

1. Beverly Wilson Palmer, ed. *Selected Letters of Lucretia Coffin Mott.* Urbana and Chicago: University of Illinois Press, 2002. 381.

2. United States Constitution: Amendment XIV. 2007. Cornell University Law School. 18 Mar. 2007 <http://www.law.cornell.edu/constitution/constitution.amendmentxiv.html>.

3. Beverly Wilson Palmer, ed. *Selected Letters of Lucretia Coffin Mott.* Urbana and Chicago: University of Illinois Press, 2002. 422.

4. Margaret Hope Bacon. *Valiant Friend: The Life of Lucretia Mott.* New York: Walker and Company, 1980. 422.

5. Beverly Wilson Palmer, ed. *Selected Letters of Lucretia Coffin Mott.* Urbana and Chicago: University of Illinois Press, 2002. 422.

6. United States Constitution: Amendment XV. 2007. Cornell University Law School. 3 Aug. 2007 <http://www.law.cornell.edu/constitution/constitution.amendmentxv.html>.

7. United States Constitution: Amendment XIX. 2007. Cornell University Law School. 18 Mar. 2007 <http://www.law.cornell.edu/constitution/constitution.amendmentxix.html>.

8. Margaret Hope Bacon. *Valiant Friend: The Life of Lucretia Mott.* New York: Walker and Company, 1980. 228–229.

9. Elizabeth A. Roslewicz. "Educating Adults through Distinctive Public Speaking: Lucretia Mott, Quaker Minister." Diss. Virginia Tech., 1999. Virginia Tech.: Digital Library and Archives. 14 Mar. 2007 <http://scholar.lib.vt.edu/theses/available/etd-042199-022852/unrestricted/chapter3a.pdf>.

10. Ibid.

INDEX

About the Author

Katie Marsico writes children's books from her home near Chicago, Illinois. She lives with her husband, Carl, and their two children, Maria and C. J. Before beginning her career as an author, Marsico worked as a managing editor in children's publishing. She dedicates this book to her daughter and son, as well as her nieces and nephews (Sarah, Frankie, Emma, Matthew, and Andrew). She has no doubt that each of them will go on to do as much good and make as many differences as did the subject of this book.

Photo Credits

Swarthmore College, cover, 3, 6, 11, 13, 14, 24, 31, 37, 52, 58, 69, 73, 91, 95, 96; North Wind Picture Archives, 17, 23, 32, 41, 81, 83, 84, 97, 99(bottom); Bridgeman Art Library/Getty Images, 42, 61, 62; AP Images, 44, 51, 88; Library of Congress/AP Images, 66, 98; Bettmann/Corbis, 71, 99 (top); Susan B. Anthony House/AP Images, 74.